Snow White
and the Seven Dwarfs

Illustrated by
Gill Guile

Brimax · Newmarket · England

Snow White lives in a big castle with her step-mother the Queen. Every day the Queen says to her magic mirror, "Mirror, mirror on the wall, who is the fairest of them all?" Every day the mirror says, "You, oh Queen, are the fairest in the land."

One day the Queen says to her mirror, "Mirror, mirror on the wall, who is the fairest of them all?" The mirror says, "You, oh Queen, are very fair; but Snow White is the fairest in the land." The Queen sees Snow White's face in the mirror. She is very angry.

The Queen tells her huntsman to take Snow White into the forest and kill her. But the huntsman lets Snow White go. She wanders through the forest until she sees a cottage. No one is at home so Snow White opens the door and goes in.

What a messy cottage it is!
Snow White decides to clean up.
She washes seven plates, seven
cups, seven knives, seven forks
and seven spoons. She dusts
seven little chairs and makes
seven little beds. Soon she is
so tired she falls fast asleep.
Seven dwarfs live in the cottage.
When they arrive home, they are
surprised to find Snow White.
They decide to let her stay.

One day, the Queen says to her magic mirror, "Mirror, mirror on the wall, who is the fairest of them all?" The mirror says, "You, oh Queen, are very fair; but Snow White, who lives in the forest with the little men, is the fairest in the land." The Queen is very angry. She decides to find Snow White.

The Queen dresses up as an old woman. She fills a basket with apples and goes to look for Snow White. The dwarfs are working in the forest. When the Queen finds their cottage she knocks on the door. "Will you buy an apple?" she asks Snow White. But this is a special apple. The Queen has put a spell on it. Snow White takes one bite and falls to the floor as if dead.

When the dwarfs arrive home, they find Snow White lying on the floor. "The wicked Queen has been here," they say sadly. The dwarfs think Snow White is dead. They make a special bed for her in the forest. All the birds and animals keep watch around her.

One day, a Prince rides through the forest. He sees Snow White lying on her bed. He says to the dwarfs, "Please let me take her home with me." As the Prince lifts Snow White up, the piece of magic apple falls from her mouth. Snow White opens her eyes. She is alive!

That day, the Queen asks her magic mirror, "Mirror, mirror on the wall, who is the fairest of them all?" The mirror says, "You, oh Queen, are very fair; but Snow White is the fairest in the land." The Queen is so angry she flies into a rage and dies. Snow White marries the Prince and they both live happily ever after.

Can you find five differences between these two pictures?